Amazing Mysteries
GONE MISSING

John Townsend

MARLBOROUGH

A⁺
Smart Apple Media

Smart Apple Media
P.O. Box 3263
Mankato, MN 56002

Printed in the United States of America

Library of Congress Cataloging-in-Publication Data

Townsend, John, 1955-
  Gone missing / John Townsend.
      p. cm. -- (Amazing mysteries)
  Includes index.
  ISBN 978-1-59920-364-5 (hardcover)
  1. Disappearances (Parapsychology)--Juvenile literature. 2. Missing persons--Juvenile literature.
  3. Curiosities and wonders--Juvenile literature. 4. Questions and answers--Juvenile literature. I. Title.
  BF1389.D57T67 2010
  363.2'336--dc22
                              2008049937

Created by Q2AMedia
Art Director: Rahul Dhiman
Designers: Harleen Mehta, Shilpi Sarkar
Picture Researcher: Amit Tigga
Line Artist: Sibi N. Devasia
Coloring Artist: Mahender Kumar

Picture credits
t=top b=bottom c=center l=left r=right

Cover Image: Q2AMedia, Inset: Q2AMedia

Insides: Digital Vision/ Photolibrary: 4, Thomas Jackson/ Getty Images: 5b, Larry St. Pierre/ Shutterstock: 9r, Jeremy Walker/ Getty
Images: 13r, Billy Black: 15t, Nara Archive: 16, Gelpi/ Shutterstock: 17, Redemption/ iStockphoto: 18m, Stephen Mallon/ Getty
Images: 19b, Nicholas Rjabow/ Shutterstock: 20t, Digital Vision/ Photolibrary: 21, Thomas Barrat/ Shutterstock: 23b, Douglas Miller/
Stringer/ Hulton Archive/ Getty Images: 24b, Sculpies/ Shutterstock: 25r, Angela Deane-Drummond/ Stringer/ Hulton Archive/ Getty
Images: 27, James Carl Wise/ Contributor/ Getty Images, 28b, David Gowans: 29t.

Q2AMedia Art Bank: 6, 7, 8, 10, 11, 12, 14, 22, 26.

9 8 7 6 5 4 3 2 1

Contents

Where Have They Gone?

People go missing all the time. They just seem to vanish. Although many soon turn up again, and others are found after a long time, some people will never be seen again. They vanish from the face of the Earth forever.

Answers?

Do people who disappear run away to start a new life? Perhaps they're unwell, need help, or just forget who they are. Were they taken? Kidnappers, murderers, or even **aliens** might have snatched them away. Did they get lost, go the wrong way, fall, or get stuck somewhere?

Can You Believe It?

A **legend** tells of James Worson, a shoemaker who lived in Leamington Spa, England. In 1873, he bet friends he could run non-stop for 8.7 miles (14 km) to Coventry. He started to run, followed by some people in horse-drawn wagons who watched to make sure James didn't cheat. During the run, he stumbled and fell with a terrible cry. People watching said James vanished before he hit the ground. He was never seen again. Nobody could ever explain what happened.

! Some people disappear and are never seen or heard of again.

A Famous Case

Farmer David Lang and his two children, George and Sarah, were playing in the front yard. David decided to walk across a field to see his horses. A family friend, Judge August Peck, came by and David turned to walk back to the house, waving to the judge. A few seconds later, David Lang—in full view of his wife, his children, and the judge—disappeared in mid-step.

Where Did He Go?

Everyone rushed to where David had been walking. They thought that he must have fallen into a hole or bog. But there was nothing there. A search by the family, friends, and neighbors revealed nothing. A few months after the disappearance, the Lang children noticed that the grass on the spot where their father vanished had turned yellow in a circle about 16.5 feet (5 m) across.

Missing File

Date: 1880

Place: Tennessee

Who: David Lang

Witnesses: Family and friend

! Some people vanish into thin air in front of witnesses.

Missing at Sea

There are many stories about ships and people that disappear forever at sea. No one knows where they have gone or can explain why they have vanished.

The *Mary Celeste*

The famous mystery of the deserted ship the *Mary Celeste* has never been solved. The ship set sail from New York in 1872, bound for Genoa in Italy.

Empty Ship

On board were its American captain, Benjamin Briggs, his wife, and their two-year-old daughter, as well as a crew of seven men. A few days after leaving New York, the *Mary Celeste* was seen drifting on the Atlantic Ocean near Portugal.

Discovery

Another American ship, the *Dei Gratia*, sailed close to the drifting *Mary Celeste*. Some of its crew climbed aboard and found the ship empty, its decks and sails wet and its lifeboat missing. There was no sign of a struggle on board the *Mary Celeste*, but all ten people who had been on the ship had vanished. They were never seen again.

! Captain Briggs, an experienced sailor, vanished with his family and crew.

Questions

Why would the captain and crew **abandon** ship? Nothing in the ship's log gave any clues. There was plenty of food and water on board. For years people have asked what happened. Did the lifeboat sink? Did they land on an island and die of thirst? Did a sea creature eat them all?

! We'll never know now what really happened on the *Mary Celeste*.

WHAT HAPPENED?

◎ Pirates? Nothing was stolen.
◎ Illness? Why would they ALL leave?
◎ Fighting? There was no blood or signs of violence.
◎ Bad weather? They'd be safer staying on board.
◎ Danger? Everything was safe and in order. The log book reported nothing unusual.

7

The *Ellen Austin*

Within 10 years of the *Mary Celeste* mystery, another ship's crew went missing. This mystery was not far from the island of Bermuda, in the area known as the Bermuda Triangle (see pages 14–17).

! The American **schooner** *Ellen Austin* often sailed from New York to London.

Ghost Ship

Captain Baker of the *Ellen Austin* saw a drifting ship with its sails flapping and masts swaying. He sent some of his crew to row over and take a look. As they climbed aboard the silent ship, the six men listened for signs of life. The lifeboats were still on the creaking, empty deck. No one was on board and nothing was out of place. There was no sign of any trouble. It was like a ghost ship. Captain Baker told his six sailors to stay on board and sail the mystery ship to the nearest port. A man called Morgan took charge.

ELLEN AUSTIN

Sailing to Land

The two ships set sail together, expecting to reach land in a few days. As night fell, thick mist drifted around them. Captain Baker lost sight of the other ship as they sailed on through the dense fog. When daylight came, the fog slowly lifted. Captain Baker looked out across the water, but there was just empty ocean as far as the eye could see. The **ghost ship** had disappeared.

Never Solved

The story, with all its mystery and legend, became yet another of the sea's dark secrets and the **fate** of the men missing in the mist has never been discovered. One story told of the mystery ship reappearing without Morgan and his crew on board. But who knows what really happened that night?

! The ghost ship was never seen again—nor were the captain and crew.

MYSTERY MOMENT

There are no lists for missing crew or casualties from the *Ellen Austin* among ships' records from the 1880s. Surely someone would have reported the names of the missing men placed on board a **derelict** ship which later disappeared?

9

The *Marlborough*

Another famous ship that disappeared was called the *Marlborough*. The mystery began when the ship set sail for London from New Zealand on January 11, 1890, with 21 people onboard. Two days later the *Marlborough* was seen by a passing **vessel**. From that time onward, the ship was never heard of again.

No News

The *Marlborough* and its crew and captain never arrived in London. After many months had passed, the ship was declared "missing," presumed sunk by icebergs near Cape Horn, at the southern end of South America. This area is known for its fierce storms and freezing weather. Everyone on board was declared dead.

Missing File

Date: 1890

Place: Off South America

Who: 21 people—captain and crew

Witness: None

! The *Marlborough* went missing in one century, and was not found until the next!

MARLBOROUGH

Discovery

The loss of the *Marlborough* was almost forgotten until 23 years later. In 1913, the crew of another ship sailing near **Cape Horn** spotted a drifter, which is a vessel that seems to be drifting aimlessly. A search party set off to climb aboard the drifter. No one was prepared for what they were about to find . . .

! Only skeletons were found on the *Marlborough* when the ship was rediscovered, 23 years after it first went missing.

EYE WITNESS

"At last we came up alongside her creaking hull. There was no sign of life on board. The mate and a number of the crew decided to board her. The sight that met their gaze was unbelievable. Below the wheel lay the skeleton of a man. Treading warily on the rotting decks, which cracked and broke in places as they walked, they encountered three more skeletons."

Unexplained

One skeleton was alone on the bridge. It may have been the captain. The remains of other bodies were found elsewhere. There was a spooky stillness all around on the ship and a smell of mold. In the captain's cabin were rotting books and a rusty sword. But the big question remained unanswered: what killed them? How had the ship remained unseen for 23 years? And why had it not smashed itself to pieces on the rocks of the South Atlantic coast?

The Flannan Isles Lighthouse

The rocky isles in the Outer Hebrides to the northwest of Scotland still hold a mysterious secret. On Eilean Mor, the biggest island, is a lighthouse. It was there, in 1900, that three men vanished without a trace.

Danger

The Eilean Mor lighthouse still flashes its light across the stormy seas to warn ships of the treacherous rocks. Today the light is automatic, and no one needs to live in this remote place to keep the lamp working. But just over 100 years ago, three lighthouse keepers lived and worked there. The rocks were said to be haunted by dead sailors who perished in shipwrecks beneath the waves.

! No one lives in the Eilean Mor lighthouse today.

Missing File

Date: 1900

Place: Eilean Mor, Scottish Island

Who: Three lighthouse keepers

Witness: None

Missing

On the day after Christmas, a small boat came to the lighthouse as it did every two weeks. It brought food and picked up one of the lighthouse keepers to take him ashore. But for the first time ever, there was no one to greet the boat. Something was wrong. The lighthouse and the island were deathly quiet. There was no flag flying and no empty boxes to collect on the **jetty**. The landing party entered the deserted lighthouse.

Inside the lighthouse the clock had stopped, the fire was out, and the three men who should have been on duty were nowhere to be seen.

Mystery

The main room in the lighthouse was clean and tidy. Food was in the cupboards and everything was just as it should have been. There were no raincoats hanging, which was strange because all three men would never go outside at the same time. In the log book two weeks before was written, "*12th December. Waves very high. Tearing at lighthouse. Storm still raging, cannot go out.*" The very last entry was three days later at 1 pm on December 15th, "*Storm ended, sea calm. God is over all.*" That was the last entry ever written by the lighthouse keepers who were never seen again.

WHAT HAPPENED?

◎ Some people say the missing men had been turned into crows by an ancient curse. Others said skeleton pirates might have carried them away. Or did aliens carry off the men? After all, **UFOs** have been reported in this part of the world. Or were all three men washed away by a freak wave? We will never know now.

The Bermuda Triangle

One area of the sea is more feared than any other. It is called the Bermuda Triangle. Airplanes and ships have entered this region between Florida, the Bahamas, and Cuba never to be seen again.

Sea of Secrets

Some sailors say the Bermuda Triangle is just a **myth**. They blame bad sailors for getting lost and not knowing about the sea's strange currents. It is a busy shipping area, so there are bound to be a few losses sometimes. But other people think differently. Why have planes gone missing here? And why is wreckage hardly ever found? There are still many unanswered questions about this sea of secrets.

The USS *Cyclops*

The USS *Cyclops* was a large cargo ship, designed to carry coal. In 1919, the *Cyclops* sailed from the United States to Brazil to refuel British ships in the south Atlantic. It set off again from Brazil, stopped briefly in Barbados, and then headed off through the Bermuda Triangle. The huge ship was never seen or heard from again. All 306 passengers and crew were gone without a trace.

! Each point of the Bermuda Triangle is about 994 miles (1,600 km) apart.

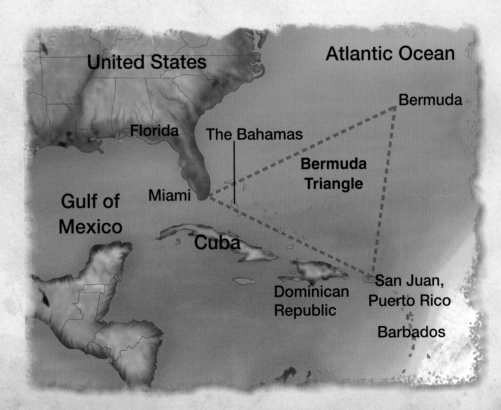

After Michael Plant set sail on his boat *Coyote*, he was never seen again.

Lost

In 1992, Michael Plant set off in his ocean racer, *Coyote*. Near Bermuda, he reported something strange. He lost electrical power and his radio began to fail. Then all radio contact was lost. Thirty-two days later, his boat was found upside-down miles away. Michael was never found. He was yet another mystery from this strange ocean.

Missing File

Date: 1992

Place: Bermuda Triangle

Who: Michael Plant

Witness: None

MYSTERY MOMENT

Perhaps time gets lost in the Bermuda Triangle. One story tells of a passenger plane disappearing from **radar** screens and the air traffic controllers feared the worst. But the Boeing 727 suddenly appeared again and landed safely 10 minutes later. The crew said they'd flown through fog and when they landed, all their clocks were 10 minutes slow!

Flight 19

One of the most famous disappearances in the Bermuda Triangle was Flight 19. The story of 27 men and six planes that vanished forever has puzzled the world for years. Where they all went and why was unknown at the end of 1945, and it still remains a mystery.

Planes in Trouble

On December 5, 1945, five Avenger **torpedo** bombers took off from the Fort Lauderdale Naval Air Station in Florida on a training flight over the sea. Charles Taylor was the officer in charge of 13 student airmen. He was in radio contact with all his fellow pilots. Over an hour into the flight, Taylor said his compass wasn't working, and he wasn't sure where he was. The weather grew worse. It was hard to see, and the pilots knew they were lost. Taylor said they should fly east, but the planes were running out of fuel and it was getting dark.

Missing File

Date: 1945

Place: Bermuda Triangle

Who: 27 men

Witness: None

! Five planes flew into the dark skies above the Bermuda Triangle . . . never to return.

No Trace

The last signal from Flight 19 back to the air base was at 7:04 p.m. After that the radios went dead. Rescue planes took off to search the area all night and through the next day. There was no sign anywhere of the five planes. Within hours of their disappearance, one of the search planes also went missing. It gave no distress signal but just vanished. There were 13 men on board, and they were never seen again.

Still Searching

Ever since 1945, people have tried to find the remains of Flight 19. In 1991, five crashed airplanes were found in deep water off the coast of Florida. But divers found the engine numbers and proved that these were not the planes from Flight 19. The final resting place of the planes and crews of Flight 19 remains one of the Bermuda Triangle's dark secrets.

WHAT HAPPENED?

◎ Flight 19 is just one of the Bermuda Triangle mysteries. There were many other training accidents here between 1942 and 1945 during World War II. Including Flight 19, 94 air crew were "lost" in total in this area. In many of the disappearances, no one really knows what happened.

! What secrets still hide in this mysterious ocean?

Vanished in America

Some people think that disappearances in the Bermuda Triangle and elsewhere may have something to do with UFOs. Do aliens kidnap humans so that they can study them? Many strange stories about people vanishing have been blamed on "creatures from beyond."

Missing File

Date: 1959
Place: Jacksonville, IL
Who: Bruce Campbell
Witness: None

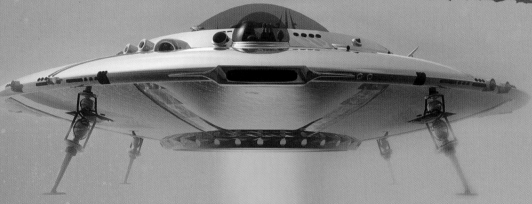

! Could aliens have kidnapped Bruce Campbell?

The Man Who Didn't Come Back

In 1959, Bruce Campbell was in bed beside his wife, Mabelita, when he disappeared. She was asleep and maybe he was, too. The Campbells were staying overnight in a hotel in Jacksonville, Illinois. Fifty-seven-year-old Bruce had driven all the way from their home in Massachusetts to visit their son and new grandson. He was very tired and was ready for bed.

Gone in His Sleep?

Twice in the night Bruce woke to ask his wife if he'd locked the car. She told him not to worry and to go back to sleep. When she woke later at 2:15 a.m., she was alone, and the space in the bed next to her was empty. A quick search found Bruce's wallet, money, shoes, glasses, keys, and all his clothes. The only things missing were the man—and the green pajamas he had worn to bed.

No Clues

Despite police searches over many weeks and a reward for anyone who could find Bruce Campbell, he was never found. No one spotted a man over 6 feet (1.8 m) tall wearing green pajamas who walked with a limp. It seems he just vanished from the face of the Earth.

WHAT HAPPENED?

◎ Did he run away to start a new life? There have never been any sightings or reports of him.
◎ Did he go sleepwalking and fall down a hole somewhere? A body has never been found.
◎ Did someone or something kidnap him? There was never a **ransom note**.
◎ Was he **abducted** by aliens?

! Did Bruce Campbell sleepwalk into nowhere?

19

! The DC-3 passenger plane was not **pressurized** like modern aircraft.

The Strange Case of Jerrold Potter

Some people really do seem to vanish into thin air. Jerrold Potter did just that—high up in the sky. In 1968, a small passenger plane took off from Kankakee, Illinois, to Dallas, Texas. It was a clear summer's day and everything on the flight was fine. Jerrold Potter told his wife Carrie that he was just going to the back of the plane to use the restroom. She never saw him again.

Where Did He Go?

After a while, Carrie grew concerned that Jerrold had been out of his seat for so long. She asked the staff to check if he was all right. But when they looked, the restroom was empty. In fact, he was nowhere on the plane. The DC-3 plane had a rear door that was open. The door didn't suck out the air from the plane, as it would in modern aircraft. A chain for keeping the door shut was found on the floor. Had Jerrold fallen out or jumped?

Missing File
Date: 1968
Place: Mid-air over the United States
Who: Jerrold Potter
Witness: None

Heavy Door

Surely Jerrold Potter didn't fall against the door and fall out? For one thing, the door had a warning in large letters "Do not open in flight." But also, it had a heavy handle that had to be turned a full circle to release two huge bolts. No one saw or heard Jerrold fall. Some passengers later said the plane shuddered slightly a few minutes after Jerrold had walked past them. It was like a bump, as if the plane went through an air pocket. But even if this had thrown Jerrold against the door, surely people would have heard him or felt a gust of wind.

WHAT HAPPENED?
◎ If he fell, would he push the door almost shut behind him?
◎ Did he make a mistake and think the exit was the restroom door—despite the notice?
◎ Was he pushed by another passenger?
◎ Did he jump on purpose without a parachute?
◎ Was he ill or confused? His wife said no.

No Reason

Jerrold Potter was a 54-year-old businessman who was happy at work and at home. He was in a good mood at the time he disappeared and in good health. There was no reason why he should suddenly throw himself from a plane. So what did happen to Jerrold Potter? A long search was made along the plane's flight path over the Ozark Mountains of Missouri. His body was never found, and the mystery remains unsolved.

! Did Jerrold Potter fall or was he pushed?

Driving Into Oblivion

Edward and Stephania Andrews were both 62 years old in 1970 when they vanished in their car. They were last seen leaving a cocktail party at the Chicago Sheraton Hotel in Illinois. The couple were both in business and lived in a fine home in the Chicago suburb of Arlington Heights.

Seemed Normal

Other people at the party said they behaved normally and seemed fine. But when they collected their car, the parking attendant thought Stephania was crying and Edward didn't look well. As he drove away, Edward scraped the car on the exit, but he kept going—heading north along the southbound lane! The attendant was the last person ever to see the Andrews.

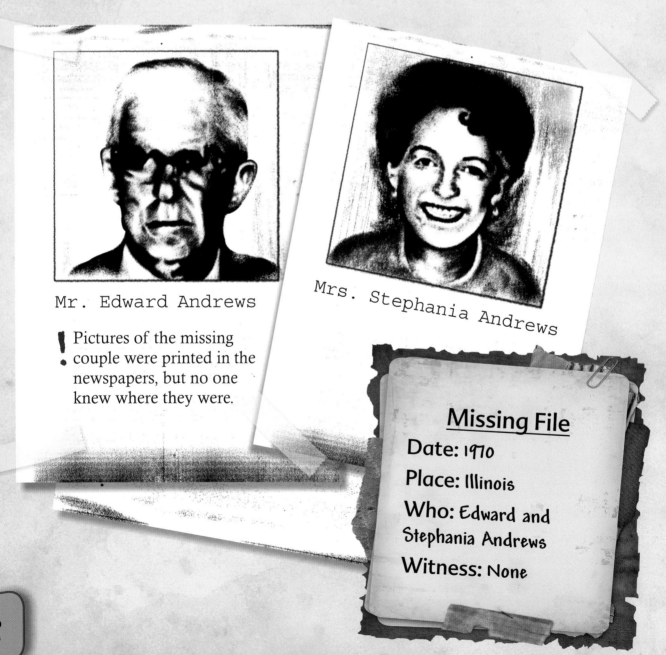

Mr. Edward Andrews

Mrs. Stephania Andrews

! Pictures of the missing couple were printed in the newspapers, but no one knew where they were.

Missing File

Date: 1970

Place: Illinois

Who: Edward and Stephania Andrews

Witness: None

They Didn't Reach Home

The following Monday, police were called to the Andrews' house when the couple were reported missing. Neither of them had appeared for work, and letters had piled up in their mailbox. Inside their house, everything was tidy, and the only items missing were the dress and jewelry Stephania Andrews had worn to the party.

Long Investigation

Why the Andrews never arrived home, and where they went, has puzzled the police ever since. The case remains open, and the police still ask for any information about the strange disappearance that night in Chicago.

WHAT HAPPENED?

◎ Maybe Edward had driven away feeling ill and plunged off a bridge into the Chicago River. But a careful search found no sign of such an accident. The river was even dredged to find the wrecked car, but nothing was found. The Andrews and their car had simply disappeared into the night, and their file remains unsolved.

! There was no sign of either the Andrews or their car in Chicago's river.

Whatever Happened to Lord Lucan?

A mystery gripped the United Kingdom in 1974. A 40-year-old man named **Lord** Lucan disappeared. There had been a murder at his home, and it looked as if he may have been the killer.

Unhappy Home

Lord Lucan lived in a nice London house with his wife and three children. But it wasn't a happy house. Sandra Rivett was the children's nanny. There were serious money problems and fights, and the marriage was all but over. Lord Lucan spent most of his time gambling at his club. But on a tragic night in November, the lives of this unhappy family hit the news. Newspapers were full of a murder story.

WOMAN FOUND DEAD

November 8, 1974

The body of a 29-year-old nanny has been found in the basement of the Lucan's home in London. Lady Lucan discovered the body last night. She ran out into the street shouting "Murder!" Police are trying to trace Lord Lucan. It seems the nanny's killer had waited in the dark basement, ready to strike. When the nanny came in to switch on the light, a pipe cracked down on her skull. Her killer bundled her into a sack. There was blood all over the room.

! A happy Lord Lucan on his wedding day.

Escape

Lady Lucan told the police how her husband had run into her bedroom covered in blood, looking shocked. Then he started hitting her. She ran from the house and raised the alarm. By the time help came, Lord Lucan had fled. The police began a hunt for Lucan right away, but he was nowhere to be found.

! Who had been waiting in the dark that night?

MYSTERY MOMENT

The nanny was due to be out that night. But she changed her mind at the last moment. Did Lucan lay in wait to kill his wife . . . and kill the wrong woman by mistake? The nanny was the same size as his wife. Who could tell them apart in the dark? The police believe Lucan did it. Why else did he run from the murder scene, never to be seen again?

Manhunt

The police searched for Lord Lucan up and down the country. They knew his car was missing, so they assumed he had driven to an airport to leave England in a hurry. After a while, the police found Lucan's blood-stained car in Newhaven on the south coast. It was thought he must have run onto a ferry and escaped across the English Channel to France.

Sightings

Seven months after Lord Lucan disappeared, a jury announced that he was guilty of murder. He became the "most wanted" man in Europe. Or had he gone to South America or Australia to start a new life? Every few days people around the world reported seeing men who looked just like Lord Lucan.

WHAT HAPPENED?

◎ Did Lord Lucan escape on a ferry? Did he get away in a speedboat? Maybe one of his friends helped him hide. Many who knew him said he could never leave his children or live in another country. Some said that he must have killed himself. But his body has never been found.

! The police discovered Lord Lucan's abandoned car—with blood inside it.

Is Lucan Alive?,

Even in the 21st century, reports appear in newspapers that Lord Lucan has been seen. One headline read: IS LORD LUCAN ALIVE IN AUSTRALIA? A British detective reported meeting Lucan while on vacation in Perth, Western Australia.

The Mystery Continues

Lord Lucan was officially declared dead in 1999. In October 2004, Scotland Yard reopened the investigation into the murder. Detectives wanted to look again at all the evidence and to use modern **DNA profiling** to try to solve the case, but they were not able to prove anything. Perhaps Lord Lucan had been a victim? Was he killed, too? We may find out one day.

! May 20, 1975: police take to the air to search for the missing Lord Lucan.

MYSTERY MOMENT

Just before he disappeared, Lord Lucan spoke to his friend, Susan Maxwell-Davis. He told her that he had tried to stop an **intruder** at his house who tried to kill his wife. This "witness" believed Lord Lucan to be innocent.

The Search Continues

The search for missing people continues for many years. One such search in 2008 was for Steve Fossett, who disappeared over the Nevada Desert in 2007.

Adventure Seeker

Steve Fossett was an American millionaire **adventurer**. He was famous for breaking all sorts of world records, including being the first person to fly solo nonstop around the world in a balloon in 2005 and 2006. In 2007, he took off in a small plane, but this time he never returned.

! Steve Fossett was famous for his exciting record-breaking travels.

Missing File

Date: 2007

Place: Nevada

Who: Steve Fossett

Witness: None

Mystery

Steve Fossett went missing on September 3, 2007 after taking off in a small aircraft from a private Nevada airstrip. All contact with him was lost, and he never returned. Despite many searches, his plane wasn't found. His wife eventually asked the courts to declare him **legally dead**, saying, "We feel now that we must accept that Steve did not survive." A police officer involved in the search admitted that Steve Fossett "may never be found." In 2008, Steve Fossett was finally declared "legally dead."

Steve Fossett soared into the sky in a plane like this . . . never to be seen again.

Who Next?

Strange cases of missing people still baffle the experts. Such mysteries have puzzled the world for years. We're left with questions, to wonder where people have gone and if they will ever be found. In the time that it's taken you to look at this book, someone else will have been reported as "gone missing."

WHAT HAPPENED?

◎ Aircraft and satellites scoured an area over 10,000 square miles (2,500,000 ha) to find Fossett's plane. In October 2008, a hiker discovered Fossett's ID cards in California's Sierra Nevada Mountains. Nearby, searchers found the wreckage of Fossett's plane, along with human remains. His disappearance was solved, but what caused the experienced pilot to crash? We might never know.

Glossary

abandon ship	an order given to the crew to leave a ship when it is in danger of sinking
abducted	to be taken away against your will
adventurer	someone who goes on dangerous and often exciting missions
alien	someone from another country—or planet
Cape Horn	the rocky southernmost tip of South America where the seas are stormy and dangerous
DNA profiling	testing the special code in each person's genes to identify patterns or types. This testing is used to discover more about evidence, such as blood or hair
derelict	left abandoned by the owner or occupants
dredge	to scrape sand and mud from the bottom of a body of water
fate	the end result or final outcome
ghost ship	a mysterious abandoned ship
intruder	someone who forcefully enters a building without permission
jetty	a small landing pier for boats
legally dead	declared as "deceased" (or dead) by law so that all paperwork can be completed
legend	a story from the past whose truth is often accepted but cannot be proven
Lord	a British title
myth	a popular belief that is passed on but that is usually false or unsupported

pressurized	kept at a normal air pressure. Modern aircraft are pressurized so that passengers can breathe comfortably at high altitude.
radar	device for detecting and locating an object by the reflection of radio waves
ransom note	a written demand from a kidnapper, usually for a payment that must be made before a captured person is released
torpedo	a long narrow bomb, often fired through water
schooner	a fast sailing ship with at least two masts and with sails
UFO	the abbreviation for unidentified flying object
vessel	a hollow container, often describing a boat, ship, or watercraft

Index

Web Finder

http://www.maryceleste.net/
Explores the mystery of the missing crew on the doomed vessel.

http://bermuda-triangle.org/
Stories about missing people and craft in the Bermuda Triangle

http://www.castleofspirits.com/strangediss.html
Stories from around the world about people who have
apparently vanished in thin air

http://www.lordlucan.com/
All about the Lord Lucan mystery